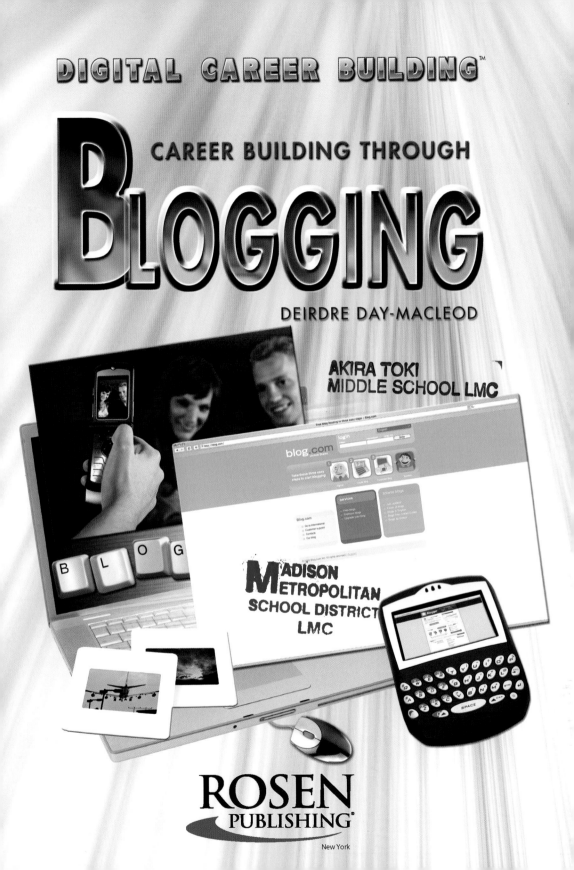

DIGITAL CAREER BUILDING™

CAREER BUILDING THROUGH

BLOGGING

DEIRDRE DAY-MACLEOD

AKIRA TOKI
MIDDLE SCHOOL LMC

MADISON
METROPOLITAN
SCHOOL DISTRICT
LMC

ROSEN
PUBLISHING®

New York

For my wired and wireless family—Dewar, Sinéad, and Rory

Published in 2008 by The Rosen Publishing Group, Inc.
29 East 21st Street, New York, NY 10010

Library of Congress Cataloging-in-Publication Data

Day-MacLeod, Deirdre.
Career building through blogging / Deirdre Day-MacLeod.
    p. cm. — (Digital career building)
Includes bibliographical references and index.
ISBN-13: 978-1-4042-1942-7
ISBN-10: 1-4042-1942-0
1. Career development—Blogs. I. Title.
HF5381.D37 2008
650.10287'67—dc22

                                                    2007000371

Manufactured in the United States of America

CONTENTS

TM

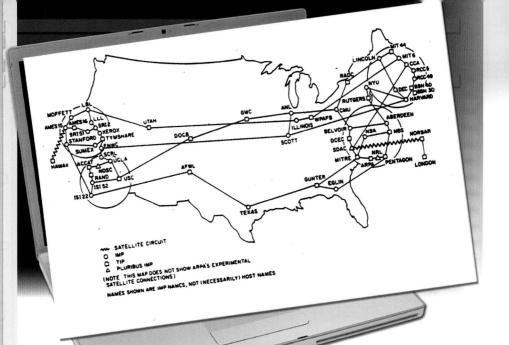

CHAPTER ONE

WHAT IS THIS BLOG OF WHICH YOU SPEAK?

Many see the birth of the Internet, in terms of its historical importance, as being equal to the invention of the printing press. "Information Revolution" has become a phrase so overused, most people don't sense the impact of the word "revolution" any longer. Readers of this book were probably born after 1983, the date most people cite as the beginning of the Internet. From that point on, almost everything about how information is gathered and sent out has been altered.

In the 1950s, when the Union of Soviet Socialist Republics (USSR) still existed, Americans feared that Communism was spreading across the world. In this Cold War environment, the Soviets launched their spaceship,

By 1977, ARPANET was linking college students all over the country.

Sputnik, making Americans afraid of being left in the technological dust. This rivalry led to the establishment of the Advanced Research Projects Agency (ARPA), which introduced a way of conveying information—packet switching. The first international packet-switched network, International Packet Switched Service (IPSS), was launched in 1978. By 1981, it included Canada, Hong Kong, Australia, Europe, and the United States.

By 1983, the National Science Foundation (NSF) had constructed a university network, later called NSFnet.

The Difference Between the Internet and the World Wide Web

The Internet is a network of networks that connects millions of computers across the globe, allowing them to communicate with each other using any of a variety of languages known as protocols. The Internet, not the Web, is also used for e-mail, which relies on SMTP, Usenet news groups, instant messaging, and FTP. So the Web is just a portion of the Internet, albeit a large portion, but the two terms are not synonymous and should not be confused.

The World Wide Web, or simply Web, is the way that people get stuff from the Internet. It is an information-sharing model that is built on top of the Internet. The Web uses the HTTP protocol, which is only one of the various protocols. The Web also utilizes browsers, such as Internet Explorer or Netscape, to access Web documents called Web pages that are linked to each other via hyperlinks. Web documents also contain graphics, sounds, text, and video.

(This date is considered by some as the start of the Internet.) In 1985, the network was made available for commercial interests. Several separate networks— including Compuserve, Telnet, Bitnet, and Usenet—had merged by the 1990s as the TCP/IP protocol became popular. The term "Internet," which meant a single global TCP/IP network, originated around this time.

As surfing became a more pleasant pursuit, what had originally been something for academics and computer buffs attracted the interest of businesspeople. We all know the names of people such as Bill Gates (Microsoft) and Steve Jobs (Apple), who have come to signify rich and successful computer tycoons, but the pivotal moments in their careers happened around the mid-1980s to early 1990s, as both envisioned the role the personal computer would play in the lives of everyday people. Entrepreneurs began establishing Web sites, basically conveying through words and images the nature of their business or organization. It became as common to give out a URL as to hand out a business card, and not having a Web site meant that you were behind the times.

 You can tell the difference between the Web site of a business, school, and non-profit by looking at the address of the site and noticing whether it is a dot-com, a dot-org, or a dot-edu.

In 1997, Jorn Barger coined the word "weblog" to describe the process of creating lists of links accompanied by short descriptions. By the following year, about thirty other sites were also calling themselves weblogs, and the

In 1997, Jorn Barger merged the words "web" and "log" into "weblog," which later became "blog."

first easy-to-use apparatus for maintaining a weblog, Pitas, was introduced. Blogger followed a month later. Prior to the creation of Pitas and Blogger, you most likely had to be a programmer to create a "blog," the shortened form of the word "weblog."

What's behind the astounding popularity of blogs? "Blog" was once a word that only nerds used; now it's overused in the mainstream media. For instance, during the midterm elections in 2006, the cable network CNN hosted a blog party and there were repeated references to the "blogosphere." Most major newspapers and magazines have hired staff bloggers, positions that didn't exist a few years ago.

According to Technorati (www.Technorati.com), which tracks Web sites, there are at least 62.5 million blogs. A July 2006 Pew study, "Bloggers: A Portrait of the Internet's New Storytellers," found that 12 million American adults keep blogs and 57 million read them.

In the online world, there are many different means of communication that involve writing. Each has its strengths and weaknesses. You've probably already used e-mail and participated in instant messaging (IMing). You may have noticed that e-mail is great when you are trying to convey information and that, for the most part, e-mails tend to be short. E-mail, like IMing and blogging, is pretty much instantaneous. E-mails are good for when you need to refer back to information, or when you are simply confirming something you've already discussed, such as "I'll see you at 7:30 at Ella's. Bring

Anatomy of a Blog

The features of a blog include the following:

- **Date header:** The date the post was written.
- **Title:** A phrase or description of the post to come.
- **Time stamp and/or permalink:** The time the post is uploaded to the blog. The time stamp often is a link to a permanent page that allows other bloggers to link it.
- **Post:** A word, sentence, paragraph, or essay, with links and names and current news.
- **Author nickname:** The name or nickname of the person who wrote the post.
- **Category:** Individual postings are often labeled as part of a category or tagged with keywords.
- **Comments:** Many blogs allow readers to leave their own comments and reactions to the author's post.

popcorn." E-mails can have one or many recipients, but you choose your audience.

IMing is generally more personal (although a growing number of businesses are using it as a means of computer conferencing). But most people don't save IMs. Unlike e-mail, both parties are present and participating in the conversation in real time.

E-mails can be retrieved at any time. So you can send your grandmother a note at 3 AM, and she can read

It's possible now to "text" your emotions and thoughts from your phone to your blog as they sweep over you.

it when she gets up at 6 AM (while you're sleeping). IMers have to be present at their computers at the same time, and the speed of their communication is limited only by their typing abilities.

Web sites are more public than either e-mails or instant messages, and they are usually designed to put forth some message into the world. Compared to the other modes of Internet communication, they resemble blogs most, although structurally they are organized differently.

A Web site is usually organized in a way that will lead you from an introductory page to other pages that contain more information, or content. Compared to a blog, which is rather vertically oriented—your eye follows the blog downward, or you click on a link and leave the site—a Web site could be considered a horizontally organized structure. Every page seems to have been created in the same moment, which could be last week or last year. The front page is sometimes updated, but not necessarily. You may return in a month and find everything just as it was. A blog, in comparison, is far more fluid. Although it may lead you back in time, it most often leads you away from itself toward other things. Web sites don't usually incorporate comments from readers, and they try their best to be "sticky," meaning that they want you to stay with them rather than surf to other sites.

Blogs existed before September 11, 2001, when terrorists attacked the United States within its own boundaries. This pivotal moment in history brought blogging to the forefront. Where other forms of communication such as telephones, cell phones, television, and radio failed,

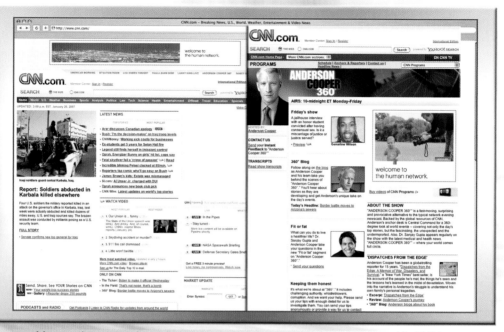

More and more traditional news organizations, such as the cable network CNN, are supplementing their news coverage with blogs. For example, Anderson Cooper's program, *Anderson Cooper 360°*, has a blog link on its Web page.

either because their technology had been damaged or because access to lower Manhattan was limited, blogs succeeded. The personal and dynamic nature of blogs gave readers insight into what was going on as it happened, including live-action photographs and video shot by witnesses. People around the world reacted to these communications and posted their feelings.

Since 2001, the growth of the blogosphere (the world or community of bloggers and blogging) has been tremendous. With bloggers located all over the world and new blogs being created constantly, you can find someone blogging about almost anything you can imagine.

The proponents of blogging consider it an agent for democracy—anyone can have a voice—while its detractors see only disorder. In some ways this argument is one about the nature of democracy itself. Those who will claim that the whole medium is degraded like to cite phrases such as "C U l8tr" as evidence that no one can spell and that the world is deteriorating rapidly. There are others who see the blogosphere as the salvation and glory of "the people," who speak the truth while the Establishment looks on. The reality is probably somewhere in between.

CHAPTER TWO
THE IMPORTANCE OF BLOGGING

When Blogger and the like were established for easy blogging, no one knew they would achieve the kind of success that they did. Today, no one has a clear idea of what lies down the road in blogging. The number of bloggers and the mainstream acceptance of blogs suggest that blogging is here to stay. But people probably thought that about the eight-track cartridge!

People speak of the dot-com boom of the 1990s as evidence of how crazy some got over something that, in actuality, generated more headlines than profits. Yet today, people read about how one company after another is acquiring this or that Web site. The business pages of the newspaper are constantly reporting on

Many friendships, and not a few romantic and professional relationships, have been created through social networking sites like Facebook, which is pictured here.

online mergers and trends. For example, will Facebook become the new MySpace? Or will it go the way of Friendster, which, although it still exists, has failed to live up to its early popularity. How much revenue can blogs generate? These are the questions that people are asking. But the Internet business is so new that the ways of measuring it are still in the formative stages.

Bloggers and Journalists

Oftentimes the idea of blogging is associated with amateurism. There are professional journalists such as Dan Rather, Katie Couric, and Anderson Cooper, and writers for newspapers and radio who have their own blogs. Then there are countless others, who sit in their pajamas and spew an endless stream of words into their computers while subsisting on coffee and enthusiasm. However, many significant news stories that the mainstream media overlooked have been broken by bloggers. Representatives of the old media have begun blogging in addition to writing for more traditional publications.

 Controversial journalist Andrew Sullivan, a former editor of the *New Republic*, began his blog, The Daily Dish (http://time.blogs.com/daily_dish/) after September 11, 2001. Sullivan remains a regular columnist for the *Sunday Times* of London.

Journalists who see blogging as a threat to their livelihoods will cite mistakes on blogs as well as clunky writing as proof that blogs are not newspapers. But this old-fashioned attitude (which many see as an attempt to

Anil Dash of Six Apart, Ltd., contributes to top print magazines while running several influential blogs and spreading the word about blogs through personal appearances.

keep journalism as a field that requires a college degree) seems to suggest that bloggers are trying to be journalists when the majority of bloggers may not see themselves that way. In fact, teenage girls are the largest blogging demographic, and a great deal of what they write reads more like a diary than an article in the *New York Times*. Most people think of blogs as repositories of words because people primarily write their blogs. Even when focusing on blogs that are mostly concerned with words, there are still a wide range of types and quite a number of bloggers who maintain different blogs for their different subjects. (For example, Anil Dash, vice president of Six Apart, Ltd., and an expert on blogging who also

For many readers, blogs such as Daily Kos (www.dailykos.com) are the most trusted sources of information about current events. Bloggers have repeatedly broken stories that the mainstream media overlooked.

writes for mainstream media such as the *New York Times*, Wired News, MSNBC, CNN, and ABC News, maintains no fewer than nine Web sites and blogs—one of which is primarily for friends and family.) Some of the word types of blogs are described below.

1. Political/opinion blogs. It is unlikely that you'll find a political blog such as Instapundit (www.instapundit. com) or Daily Kos (www.dailykos.com/) delving into extremely personal details like their struggles with friends and family, or ruminating on the kind of laundry detergent most likely to remove that ketchup from their favorite T-shirt. But you will often find

that bloggers, even the more journalistic ones, are more likely to reveal themselves online than in print. These are the most well-known blogs because they get the most publicity. Many political blogs display their leanings in ways that supposedly impartial journalists do not. Many, like Arianna Huffington's blog, www.HuffingtonPost.com, are written by a group of similarly oriented individuals.

The instantaneity of blogging gives bloggers a way to get the word out without having to shout "Stop the presses!" A number of writers, such as Ana Marie Cox of Wonkette and Julie Powell, whose book, *Julie and Julia: 365 Days, 524 Recipes, 1 Tiny Apartment Kitchen*, was published in 2005 by Little Brown and Company, skipped the print medium entirely and began as bloggers. Such speed lends itself to certain kinds of reporting, including gossip, local news, and political revelations and rants.

One of the most popular sports blogs on AOL isn't run by a professional blogger, sportscaster, or even someone with years of gathering sports wisdom, but by a twelve-year-old from Detroit. Nick Barnowski's Sports Nut's Sports Blog has been named AOL's Sports Blog of the Week and has gained national attention. Once he's finished with middle school, high school, and college, Nick would like to become a professional sportswriter. (Posted on September 3, 2006.)

2. Diaries and journals. By far the largest category of blogs is the online diary. Writers of these blogs give regular accounts of their lives. The best of

Julie Powell's blog, the Julie/Julia Project, about preparing meals from Julia Child's best-selling tour de force, *Mastering the Art of French Cooking*, landed her a book contract.

these allow the reader to follow a story that unfolds like a soap opera but is real. The worst are dull and of no interest to anyone other than the writer (and maybe the writer's parents or employer).

3. Hobby blogs. In blogs devoted to interests or hobbies, the writer has channeled all his or her enthusiasm for something into a blog about that pursuit. No matter how eccentric you think your interest is, someone in cyberspace has a more off-the-wall enthusiasm. Back in the olden days, if you liked something no one else cared about, you might feel like you were a freak, or at the very least, alone. You may be chagrined to find out that you aren't as unique in your love of nineteenth-century dollhouses as you thought you were, but you will learn some new things and possibly strike up a friendship with others who share your enthusiasm.

4. Gadget blogs. A great deal of these blogs are, as one might expect, devoted to computer technology and gadgetry. You can find blogs that focus on a specific cell phone model as easily as those that devote themselves to the love of celebrities such as Josh Hartnett or Britney Spears.

 Gizmodo (www.gizmodo.com) includes a gadget guide on its blog that includes helpful information on laptops, cell phones, PCs, software, and digital cameras, among other equipment.

Need to know what you need to buy? Gizmodo (www.gizmodo.com) keeps readers up to date on the latest in gadgetry and techno-toys.

5. Local blogging (or hyper-local). One way that blogs have filled a void is by focusing on what was only reported in local newspapers. A blogger can attend a town hall meeting and give the salient details immediately. (If there is wireless communication, a blogger can write it as it happens.) Interested persons can tune in and, if the blog enables comments, express their opinions. The information that might be of no interest to someone half a mile down the road, such as what traffic is like right now on the corner of Washington and Main streets, might be of vital importance to someone thinking about getting home in time to catch a favorite TV

show. Think about how much happens in your school or town that never becomes "news," but could if someone were there to document it.

6. Gossip/celebrity blogging. Blogging has lent itself to gossip. One of the most popular blogs, Gawker (www.gawker.com), devotes much of its content to rumors about celebrities in New York City, even to the point where readers can post when they see someone famous or visit a site map that pinpoints the location of the relevant celebrity. For example, it's reported that Paris Hilton was seen shopping for baubles in Bloomingdale's at Fifty-ninth Street and Lexington Avenue.

 **AOL Red (http://teens.aol.com/) includes celebrity and gossip blogs for teens who like to chat about rumors and celebrity reports.**

It's probably safe to say that whatever you are interested in, someone somewhere is writing a blog about it. If they aren't, it's time you filled the gap.

Honeymoon

Abby in front of some building.

182 photos | Detail view

CHAPTER THREE

OTHER WAYS TO BLOG TOWARD A FUTURE

U p until this point, we've talked about blogs as primarily composed of words. If you want to be a writer, the transition between the screen and the page seems logical. But, as you have probably already noticed, people aren't just writing online anymore. Blogging has ventured beyond written words into the spoken word and to images both moving and still. This translates into a dizzying array of possibilities that's expanding the blogosphere in new directions.

Some people grew up having to learn how to develop their own film (which meant using lots of chemicals in a darkroom) or waiting for other people to do it for them. Either way, you wouldn't know what you'd got until well

Sites like Flickr (www.flickr.com) and Shutterfly (www.shutterfly.com) allow readers to post their personal and professional images.

after the pictures had been taken. (The Internet term WYSIWYG—what you see is what you get—did not apply to this form of picture making.) If you could do your own developing, you had a chance to manipulate the image, but otherwise you had to wait until the photos were processed to see them. Today, digital photography allows you to see what you are getting as soon as you've snapped it. You can upload the image onto your computer from your digital camera (or camera phone) and then play around with it to make it larger, give it more contrast, or get rid of the things you just don't like in the picture. A camera with decent resolution can be purchased for less than $100, and the software to edit and resize your photos can be downloaded for free. Your photos can be posted online almost instantaneously.

One of the most exciting developments in blog-land was the development of visual sites such as Flickr, which was bought by Yahoo! in March 2005 for $35 million, and YouTube, which was in existence for only eighteen months when Google acquired it for $1.65 billion.

QUICK TIP Flickr allows users to upload twenty megabytes of photos for free and to easily share and annotate them.

Although you could create a photoblog through other Web hosts, the advantage of a Web host designed specifically for photographs is that it offers extra features such as the ability to annotate and tag images, and to work with images from other sources, including the New York Public Library. The search function gives you access to two million photos, which, as long as you abide

Creative Commons

Creative Commons, a tax-exempt charitable organization, allows people who create works to share their work online without losing the ownership of their creations. To avoid the problems that copyright laws written in a pre–www age have had in controlling the spread of content, Creative Commons seeks to find a means to guard both free expression and the rights of authors. Through the Creative Commons, authors can obtain licenses that allow them to release their work on the Web by choosing the type of license that best suits their work. Creative Commons also provides metadata descriptions of the license and the work, making it easier to automatically process and locate licensed works. Lawrence Lessig, the chairman of the board of Creative Commons, argues in his book *Free Culture* (2004) that people live in "a culture in which creators get to create only with the permission of the powerful, or of creators from the past." Lessig believes that the Web has the potential to undermine the monopoly that traditional content distributors have held over popular music and popular cinema.

by Creative Commons' attribution rules, you may use freely. Creative Commons is a tax-exempt charitable organization that allows people who create works to share them online without losing ownership of them. People can obtain licenses that allow them to release their work on the Web by choosing the type of license that best suits their needs.

YouTube basically performs the same function for moving images that Flickr does for stills, and, like Flickr,

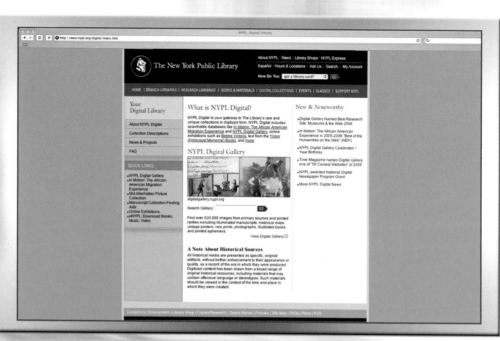

The image search function of the New York Public Library (www.nypl.org) gives you access to two million photos, which you can use as long as you abide by Creative Commons rules.

the vast majority of the content comes from amateurs. But you can also "vlog" through other sites. Sources for video clips that are short and easily uploaded and downloaded onto such devices as iPods include the news, sports, music videos, television shows, film trailers, and home movies. The practice of blogging clips is known as vlogging, just as photographic blogging is called photoblogging.

Audioblogging

Audio blogs allow you to create and publish audio files. You can narrate your life in your own voice or play DJ. Since the beginning of 2003, MP3 blogs have become increasingly popular. The rise of audioblogging has led to

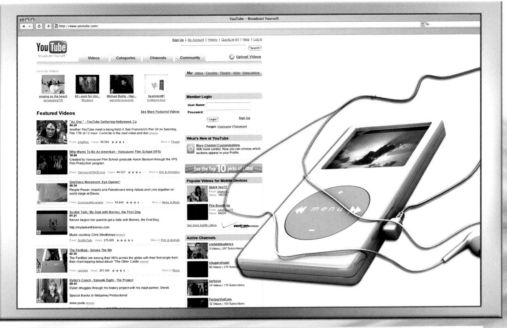

YouTube (www.youtube.com) allows you to surf through home videos, old TV clips, last night's favorite TV program, music videos, and almost anything else that has been committed to film.

podcasting, which is named for Apple's ubiquitous MP3 player. A podcast is simply an audio track that can be downloaded and played at will. It's like a radio that you can play through your computer and/or transfer to a portable MP3 player.

A blogcast is a podcast that comes with words and can be indexed and searched. The medium is a hybrid of blogging and radio. Podcasts can be recordings of lectures, walking tours, comedy acts, books, and, of course, music.

Music Blogs

Many independent music labels, public relations agencies, and recording artists have seen the value of online publicity. They now send free copies of their CDs to MP3 blogs.

 Among the first widely known MP3 blogs were Stereogum (www.stereogum.com) and Fluxblog (www.fluxblog.org). Stereogum was

Clips Made Them Famous . . .

In 2005, two Chinese students, Huang Yixin and Wei Wei, now known as the Back Dorm Boys displayed their lip-synching talents by mugging to a song by the Backstreet Boys. The two instantly became famous as the video gained notoriety online. Not only did they appear on television after their video became popular, but they also got a contract to represent Motorola's cell phones in China as well as on Sina.com, one of the largest Chinese Internet portals.

David Elsewhere's dance performance that featured his abilities at popping and liquiding, two fancy dance maneuvers, at the 2001 Kollaboration Competition spread so widely over the Internet that he was hired to appear in commercials for Heineken, iPod, Pepsi, and other companies.

The Back Dorm Boys, Huang Yixin and Wei Wei, became famous for lip-synching.

established in 2002 and covers indie rock bands as well as pop star gossip. Fluxblog, which was created in 2002, offers a mix of music but focuses primarily on current rock and pop. Comments on music and the music industry are also found there.

Major labels have come to see blogs as a way to stimulate "word of mouth" attention for smaller acts. For instance, in 2004, Warner Brothers allowed the blog Music (For Robots), at http://music.for-robots.com, to post an MP3 by the rock band the Secret Machines. In early 2005, Music (For Robots) was featured on MTV because of how it had drawn attention to the Hysterics, a band made up of four fourteen- and fifteen-year-olds from Brooklyn.

Moblogging

Bloggers aren't necessarily sitting at their desks, or even near their computers. More of the blogging platforms are collaborating with cell phone companies to allow you to post from your blog wherever you are. With a cell phone equipped with a camera (many have video capability as well), it's possible to instantaneously publish wirelessly. All it takes to make the private public—to make the world aware of abuse (such as the treatment of prisoners of war) or just to show everyone how it looked from your seat in the second row of the concert—is technical know-how and a cell phone.

Mapblogs

A new development in visual blogging has been map-blogging. This online social community lets you

With www.flickr.com/photos/tags/cellphone, you can use your cell phone to send photos of cell phones (or anything else that is where you are) straight to your Flickr.com page.

bookmark and annotate real-world locations. You can Blog geographically through Flickr or through such sites as Wayfarer and Flagr, which allow you to group, share, and discuss locations under a common theme or idea. Your summer vacation can become a mapping experience, complete with annotations and tags. Put a map on a blog, and every reader can check in with his or her location. It's amazing to see how far-flung your audience might be.

Bloggers can be photographers, filmmakers, dancers, or even geographers, and they can use their blogs to gain at least some degree of attention for their talents. Generally, if you make money, it's because you gained attention, which can lead you to other venues. You can take advertising and get paid by the hit, but don't expect the millions to roll in! If you take your blogging seriously, whether you reap the benefits financially or not, the experience is sure to serve you in your future.

CHAPTER FOUR

WHAT DO YOU WANT FROM YOUR BLOG?

There are a million different ways to approach your blog. Spend some time thinking about what kind of blog you want and what you seek to gain from keeping a blog. According to Pew's July 2006 study of the Internet, the primary reason people state for beginning to blog is a desire to express themselves. Other reasons include the pursuit of learning, connections with others, and the creation of a portfolio of work that may lead to other things—either within cyberspace or in the real world.

Everything you do online is public, even when it seems private. Anyone can adopt a screen name and a persona. Just because Sweet16Kansas has that name

Publishing a blog allows the world to glimpse aspects of your personality that you never showed before.

doesn't mean that he or she isn't a fifty-year-old who lives in Chicago. The Internet can be seductive, and it can make you feel as though you are connecting with kindred spirits. You can easily find yourself in conversations with people you would never speak to if you met them on the street. Never give away your location, name, or information that could be used to find you in real life.

The Diary Blog

Do you feel comfortable telling the world about your personal life? Remember that the things you post will always be somewhere and anyone (including your mother, the admissions office at the college of your choice, and an employer) can read them. Although you can choose at some point to take down the blog, that doesn't guarantee that it hasn't been saved elsewhere in cyberspace. Pulling back your words once they've been out in cyberspace is next to impossible. So take the time to consider whether or not you are willing to tell your deepest, darkest secrets to the whole world.

If you are, but you don't want anyone to know, you can easily assume a name. (Of course, a hacker or reasonably adept computerista could still figure out what your real name is, but most people won't take the time or don't have the skills to embark on the task of unmasking you.) Anonymity provides a nice cloak, but it won't make you famous (or provide you with a portfolio to reference).

Expression

People generally express themselves daily in other ways, so why do they need to blog? For many, the idea of

AOL's attempt to capture some of MySpace's teen market is the blog Red.com (http://red.blogs.aol.com), whose home page is seen here.

actually putting effort into a blog can kill the urge early on. You may walk around all day seeing brilliant ideas, but when it comes to actually creating the sentences or assembling the links, you suddenly find that you've got brain freeze.

The glory of the blog is that you can talk about how you feel about the world, and for some reason, publicly sharing your beliefs feels good. Look at AOL's new teen blog, AOL Red, or sift through blog entries at MySpace or any number of popular blog-hosting sites. You'll find tons of angst and soap-operatic shenanigans, but you will also find some truly hilarious stories and some that are inspiring.

With more than 50 million accounts, the majority of which belong to users between the ages of fourteen and twenty-four, MySpace (www.myspace.com) gets more page views per day than any site on the Web except Yahoo!

It's fine to write down the minute details of your daily life, and if you are a really good writer, you can make even the most banal of your activities interesting. Being a good writer means many of the things it has always meant: show, don't tell; use language that is vivid and alive; be clear; and avoid clichés and redundancies. Online writers try to show personality. Even blogs that are less personal in terms of subject matter are filled with personal touches, whether they're coming through in the voice, style, or design. Blogs that are collaboratively written, such as BoingBoing: A Directory of Wonderful Things (www.boingboing.net) and Huffington Post (www.huffingtonpost.com), seem to exude a group

THE HUFFINGTON POST.

Opinions proliferate online. Blogs such as the Huffington Post (www. huffingtonpost.com) have brought attention to writers on the left side of the political spectrum.

personality by keeping their points of view and style despite their dependence on multiple posters.

Learning About Other Things

The best blogs make use of links to other blogs and Web sites. When you are chronicling your daily life, you can find ways to turn outward rather than making the blog all about you. For instance, you work as a paperboy and you were bitten by a dog. Once you've gone through all the stuff about how annoying it is that those people haven't trained little Fifi to behave, you could start thinking about dog bites in general. How many people get bitten every day? When are bites more likely to occur?

What breeds of dogs bite most often? Through a wiki, you can gain access to a host of studies on dog bites and their medical treatment. The wiki may then direct you to sites where original research has been published by scientists and doctors studying dogs and bites.

Within the space of a few Googles (or Dogpiles, or whatever search engine appeals to you most), you'll have learned a bunch of things. Your own experience will have been enriched by all the knowledge you've gained.

According to some (who extrapolate from Moore's Law, which primarily concerns computer memory), the world's collective knowledge doubles every eighteen months. Even if this were the case, without power to access all this new knowledge, a great deal of that learning would be inaccessible to most people. With the rise of "wikis" like Wikipedia, each reader is also the editor and, with the writer, can correct mistakes and contribute what he or she knows about the subject. (Wiki comes from the Hawaiian word "wiki-wiki," which means "quick.") Although Wikipedia, the collaborative online encyclopedia that is the best known of the Web's wikis, is often considered an unreliable source, studies have found that its rate of error is only slightly higher than that of the *Encyclopedia Britannica*. In addition, unlike conventional sources of information, a wiki is dynamic and ever changing. The first reports of the giant tsunami that hit South Asia in December 2004 appeared first as a paragraph posted within hours of the great wave hitting the beach. Within forty-eight hours, the entry had grown to pages and pages of information, both scientific and personal. There is no other source of

Wikis have made knowledge a collaborative experience. "Wiki-wiki" is the Hawaiian word for "quick," and information arrives on Wikipedia (http://en.wikipedia.org/wiki/Main_Page) almost as fast as it happens.

information that can provide such knowledge so quickly.

Rules of Blog Writing

The following are some helpful guidelines for writing your blog:

1. Take time to write well. Make your words speak as clearly and vividly as possible.
2. Let your personality show through. People like seeing glimpses of humanity in blogs.
3. Brevity is important. Most blog posts that are longer than a few lines just don't get read.

4. Clarity. What seems obvious to you may appear complicated to someone who does not share your experiences. Imagine that your reader is an alien or your baby brother.

5. Before posting, read your words over and then read them again to make sure that your writing makes sense. Reading aloud may seem absurd when you are sitting in an empty room, but your ear is sometimes smarter than your eye.

6. Frequent posting is essential. Post regularly or you will leave your readers stranded and probably annoyed. They are fickle, and they will disappear quickly.

7. Safety above all else. No matter how careful you are—and careful means never giving out any personal information to strangers, and personal means anything that might allow someone to find you—you may encounter things online that are offensive. Even the most restrictive filters don't catch everything. Everything you post online will be online and available to strangers. If you blog through MySpace, AOL Red, or one of the blogging services that enable you to keep messages within your network, you are safer, but you also forgo the potential to make useful connections beyond people you already know. If you have an open blog that allows comments—and you can always disable the comment function—you will receive spam and you may find that while many people are supportive and kind, many are also annoying and sometimes abusive.

8. Learn to click the back button when you stumble upon something you don't want to see.

9. Do not respond to comments that do not seem well intentioned.

10. Set your blog with a screen name so that any e-mail sent to you goes to an address that is not your primary e-mail account.

11. Whenever you post anything, think about how you would feel if your grandmother saw it. Think about how you might feel if the thing popped up in five or ten years. Even if disabled, your blog information never completely disappears from the Web. It could show up when employers, college admissions officers, and others do a search. If you express negative opinions, the people about whom you are complaining may stumble on your comments.

12. Take three deep breaths or count to ten before pressing the send button. Think of your posts as being similar to tattoos that leave indelible, though not always obvious, marks.

Networking

As you find others who are interested in the same subjects as you are, comment on their blogs and refer them to yours. Make a practice of giving your blog address as part of your e-mail sign off. You might be moved to write to that paperboy in Tokyo or to comment on the blog of a mail carrier in Detroit, Michigan, thereby forging a connection that extends beyond your own life. You may, in turn, send links to your posting to these other people (without revealing anything too personal about yourself, of course). Someone might read your post and write about his or her experience with that nasty pit bull down the block. A lover of pit bulls might explain that they are sweet animals and only bite bad people or were abused in the past. A discussion might ensue about adopting abused dogs versus getting only puppies. In no time, a dialogue has occurred. Someone with a bigger site might notice your blog and link to it. When you get linked to by a more popular site, your own rank goes up. (It's not unlike how things work in the lunchroom at school: if the most popular kid decides to sit next to you, you immediately rise a few notches on the cool kid charts.) There is no bad linking, so even if the dorkiest blog in all of cyberspace links to you, a link is a link and can't really hurt.

Blogging has become a means toward many ends. The stories of how so-and-so got discovered have almost become urban legends, although many of these tales are true. You can get discovered through your blog, but it won't happen without work.

Although the majority of bloggers may not be in the game to advance their careers, perhaps they ought to be. A number of people have found fame and fortune via a blog, many of them completely without trying. More have made smaller, but still significant, progress toward achieving their goals.

If you aren't that excited about blogging, but you really want to get a book contract or record deal, your approach may be slightly different from someone who blogs for the love of blogging. Whether you see your blog

The sportsblog, including the one found on http://sportsillustrated.cnn.com, gives Monday-morning quarterbacks the opportunity to argue with professional journalists about football games.

as a means to show the world that you are ready for that job at *Sports Illustrated,* or to demonstrate your superior design skills, it makes sense to be clear in advance about what you expect to gain from your blog.

Blogging Toward a Career

The most obvious careers that you can prepare for by blogging involve writing. That print journalists have been so defensive about the growth of blogging points to the fact that much of what they do for a living is being done by people who do not have journalism credentials. You can also set yourself up as a reviewer by focusing your blog on the discussion of books, movies, technology, or whatever strikes your fancy. Moreover, you can publish your fiction and other creative writing on your blog. As a fiction writer, poet, or memoirist, your ability to publish yourself will give you a far greater chance of getting that book contract than keeping your precious pages in the bottom of a drawer.

Photojournalists, filmmakers, animators, and the like can create their online portfolios, but so can actors, comedians, dancers, and burgeoning newscasters. In fact, fine artists, cabinetmakers, and craftspeople could also post photographs of their work. Anyone who makes anything that involves some product that can be seen or heard can consider the Web as a means of gaining publicity.

 Although social networks such as MySpace might seem like a great place to display photos, they aren't the ideal places for serious photographers to show their work. Most places limit the overall size and number of photos that can be uploaded. Perhaps a better solution for photo portfolios is to join a photo-sharing group and then link your photo display to your profile. Prior to choosing a photoblog site, visit the following directories: www.photoblogs.org, DMOZ Directory of Photoblogs (dmoz.org/Arts/Photography/Weblogs/Photoblogs), and/or Yahoo Photoblogs (dir.yahoo.com/Computers_and_Internet/Internet/World_Wide_Web/Weblogs/Photography).

As you consider what career you want, you may realize that through blogging you don't have to wait to grow up to get started in that field.

CHAPTER FIVE

PUTTING YOURSELF OUT THERE

Chances are that you won't receive national attention for your first blog. You may not even get that many hits. You might blog for months and only gather a handful of readers. But if you are diligent and do everything you can to publicize your blog, and your blog is interesting to enough people, you will probably gain a sizeable audience. At the very least, you'll be able to give people an address to find your work.

Before you begin blogging, decide what your goals are in this respect. For some, friends, family, and the occasional drop-in blogger are sufficient for them. Others crave more. To get there, though, you have to work at it. Consider following these five helpful rules while blogging:

Blogger (www.blogger.com) provides easy guidelines for creating a blog and helping you organize it.

Rule 1: Blogging takes time and dedication.
At first glance, the whole blogging thing might appear effortless, but it's not. According to a study of bloggers conducted by the University of Massachusetts, 31 percent of bloggers spend one to four hours per day doing research for and writing their posts, whereas 65 percent spend less than one hour. The study concluded that: 1) blogs take time; 2) blogs should be planned; 3) blogging is about interaction; and 4) the writing in a blog should be clear, real, focused, and above all, interesting.

Rule 2: Plan your blog.
When deciding what you want your blog to be, look at the blogs that are already out there. Study them so that you can see what appeals to you and what turns you off.

Many blog hosts provide templates so that you can choose a design without any knowledge of HTML (the basic programming language for blogs). You can begin this way, but you may find that down the line you'll want to add to it or alter it. Changing isn't too difficult, and the ability to personalize your blog will require less technological skill as time goes on.

If you are showcasing your talent as a Web designer, you don't want to use the same old template that is at the top of the Blogger list. For most people, until the HTML flows freely (which may never happen), it's probably best to stick to one of the tried-and-true designs that are supplied for your use. You may also learn the basics of HTML tagging and start to play around a bit with colors, fonts, and the like. As you grow more comfortable, you'll tweak it here and there.

Before beginning their own blogs, many new bloggers take time to look at all the choices available to them.

But starting out, just take on someone else's style and make it your own.

However, decide right away on what page elements you would like. Do you want a sidebar to show your favorite sites? Do you want to include a profile or a photograph? How will you describe your blog?

 If you decide to play around with the template, make a copy of the old one or you'll have to re-create it if things go awry. Some things do have a tendency to happen unexpectedly in cyberspace!

Are the blogs you like written by one or many people? What kind of voice is the writer using? Is she personal or more distant?

By sharing the workload with others, you can take days off without worrying about stranding your loyal readership.

What does the blog focus on? How often is it updated?

You'll get a sense of how much time you'll be spending by noting the frequency of posts. By going to a blog-tracking site (such as Technorati) you can also get a report on the popularity of the blog.

How long is the average post? Is it a few paragraphs or a few sentences? Does the writer mostly use links, or are there lots of personal flourishes? How many links does each post contain? Many diary-like blogs won't have links. But without links you deny yourself some of the most exciting things about blogging and limit your own readership.

Sites like Technorati (www.technorati.com) monitor the popularity of blogs, tracking links, hits, and other data.

Consider your own reaction to the blog. Did you want to know more? Did you click on the links? If you did, did you return?

Did you think about bookmarking or tagging the blog?

As you plan how to approach your blog, it's important to set the tone early. Blog readers tend to crave consistency. Just as a book reader expects to read a mystery when there are all the clues on the cover—a gun, a private eye, a beauty in distress—your blog readers will have expectations based on how you present yourself. If you begin posting twenty times every day and then take a month off, you will lose and alienate your readers. Some check at regular intervals for new posts, and they will expect you to maintain consistency.

Rule 3: Link a lot.
The more you link, the more you are likely to be linked to. If you comment on other people's blogs, you can provide a link to your own blog. If you love the work of someone else and say so, it's only natural that the person will want to find out more about you. Likewise, you will be tempted to find out more about your fans.

Rule 4: Be easy to find.
Make sure to list your blog on such sites as Technorati, Blogbuzz, or BlogExplosion. These sites will track your hits and sometimes make a "ping" sound, helping readers to know when they have new material.

Once people start linking to your blog or putting your blog on their blogrolls (list of favorites), you'll get more visitors. It's sort of a thrill to have some blogger you admire decide to admire you back. The more it happens, the more popular you are.

Some blogs will have a box with tags in it; some words will be large and others small. A meme box displays the words that occur most frequently in the blog—the size of the word indicates its frequency in the blog. Tagging is simply a description of what the post is about. For instance, a post about a roving pack of wombats attacking senior citizens in Cleveland could be tagged in various ways. You might emphasize the wildlife angle or the fact that incidents occurred in Cleveland. You may have already encountered meme maps—those blocks of words

One of the ways bloggers push traffic is by registering their blogs on sites like BlogExplosion (www.blogexplosion.com), which helps readers find the blogs that suit their interests.

in all different sizes to indicate their frequency on someone's blog page. By deciding what the important facts of your own post and someone else's are, you make it easier for others to find useful material. But you also participate in the classification of information.

The way a zoologist might understand the story as opposed to a senior citizen health-care organization could be quite different. When you tag the sites you read, you add another layer to the community of taggers. You make the vast amount of online information easier to negotiate. In the same way that a wiki invites the participation of readers, tagging gives you the opportunity to evaluate and sort data.

If you have a connection to a social networking site such as Del.cio.us, you could see who else tagged the same article and find out what each reader tagged. Thus you might find out that there has been a horrible upsurge in wombat violence, or that senior citizens in Cleveland are suffering from a host of other problems in addition to wombats. Your preferences will lead you in the direction that you want to go, pulling you deeper into the Web and adding to a communal knowledge base. Instead of each person being interested in the subject beginning from nowhere and having to slog through article after article, you are given access to the work others have done. In return, you share your own work.

Tagging on such sites as Triggernet, YouTube, and MySpace, among others, adds a whole new level of inter-activity to blogging. Tagging is similar to an index that allows readers to know not only what you are writing about, but also what the subjects are for your visual images on Flickr and even the style of music (for example, as in the Music Genome Project [http://www.pandora.com/mgp.shtml]).

Rule 5: Write well.
According to Ana Marie Cox, whose Washington gossip blog, Wonkette, led to her becoming the Washington editor for *Time* magazine and a couple of book deals, she put things up twelve times per day on her blog. According to Cox in a *New York Times* article in 2006, the secrets to success are that a blogger should have a "strong, defined personality with a sense of humor about themselves, an ability to filter news quickly, and to recognize what is

interesting to other people, as well as interesting to themselves and finding the balance between those things."

This is an amazing moment in the history of communications. Sometimes the speed at which things are changing can be overwhelming as well as exciting. So much of how you shape your future—no matter how you imagine it to be—depends on how you respond to change and how you are able to position yourself in relation to a dynamic and ever-expanding world of information and expression. Blogging is one way for you to express yourself, but it is also a way for you to find yourself and others like you. As you embark on your blog journey, ask yourself, "Why am I doing this?" You can change your goal the moment you outgrow it, but having something to look forward to will inspire and direct you. No one knows what kinds of careers will exist in twenty or thirty years, but keeping yourself alive and active will put you in the best position to make your future the best possible.

GLOSSARY

audioblog A blog composed of posts that are mainly voice recordings.

blogger One who runs a blog. Also Blogger.com, a popular blog hosting site.

blog host A company offering the tools with which to create and maintain a blog.

blogosphere The worldwide community of blogs.

blogroll A list of blogs. A blogger features a list of his or her favorite blogs in the sidebar of his or her blog.

content The stuff that makes up a blog—words, photos, etc.—excluding the design and other fixed structural components.

feed Also blog feed, webfeed, or RSS. A way of delivering and syndicating blog posts or summaries so that they arrive directly in a browser.

hit A request for a Web page.

HTML (hypertext markup language) The language that composes a Web site.

metadata Data about data. Metadata describes specific information about the data; for example, who collected it, how it is formatted, and when and how it was collected

moblog Combination of the words "mobile" and "blog." A moblog features posts sent via cell phone or mobile phone.

permalink Permanent link; the unique URL of a single post.

photoblog A blog consisting primarily of photo-graphic images.

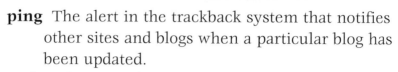
ping The alert in the trackback system that notifies other sites and blogs when a particular blog has been updated.

podcasting Combination of "iPod" and "broadcasting." An audio file often formatted like a program that can be downloaded and played on a computer or MP3 player (such as an iPod).

trackback A system that enables a blogger to view who has seen his or her original post and has written about it. The system works by sending a ping between the blogs, and therefore providing the alert.

vlog A video blog.

wiki A collaborative endeavor where everyone has the ability to create and edit entries on a range of topics.

WYSIWYG (what you see is what you get) A way of editing HTML so that it shows what you will get rather than just displaying code.

A Sampling of the Blogosphere

This list is by no means exhaustive. How could it be with millions of blogs appearing all the time? However, it does provide you with some blogs that will probably be around for a while. Be sure to look at the sidebars of blogs you like so that you can find out what blogs those bloggers are reading. To see who is most popular, go to Technorati.com.

Blogs about blogging and other technological issues:
A List Apart: www.alistapart.com
Make zine: http://makezine.com/blog
Techcrunch: www.alistapart.com

Culture and art:
Artopia: www.artsjournal.com/artopia
Arts & Letters Daily: http://aldaily.com
Design Observer: www.designobserver.com
Drawn—The Illustrators and Cartoonist's Blog:
  http://drawn.ca

Generally interesting/gadget oriented:
BoingBoing: www.boingboing.net
Gizmodo: www.gizmodo.com

Gossip/celebrity:
Defamer: www.defamer.com
Gawker: www.gawker.com

MollyGood: www.mollygood.com
RadarOnline: http://radaronline.com

Music:
Fluxblog: www.fluxblog.org
Moby.com: www.moby.com
Stereogum: www.stereogum.com

Politics:
Crooks and Liars: www.crooksandliars.com
Daily Dish: www.andrewsullivan.com
Daily Kos: www.dailykos.com
Wonkette: www.wonkette.com

Sports:
Sports Blogs: www.sportsblogs.org
Sports Frog: www.sportsfrog.com
True Hoop: www.truehoop.com
Yanksfan vs. Soxfan: yanksfansoxfan.typepad.com/ysfs

Writing/publishing:
Blog of a Bookslut: www.bookslut.com/blog
GalleyCat: www.mediabistro.com/galleycat
Literary Saloon: www.complete-review.com/saloon
Maud Newton: www.maudnewton.com/blog

Blog Tools
Blog hosts:
Blogger: www.blogger.com
LiveJournal: www.livejournal.com
MySpace: www.myspace.com
TypePad: www.typepad.com

Blog feeds and feed searches:
Feedster: www.feedster.com
Newsgator: www.newsgator.com
Pubsub.com: www.pubsub.com

Blog lists:
Bloglines Most Popular: www.bloglines.com/topblogs
Feedster Top 500: http://top500.feedster.com
Technorati's Top 100: www.technorati.com/pop/blogs

Blog search engines:
www.logarama.com
www.Blogwise.com
www.Daypop.com

Readers and subscribers:
Blogarithm: www.blogarithm.com
BlogsNow: www.blogsnow.com/
Weblogs.com: www.weblogs.com

Web Sites

Due to the changing nature of Internet links, Rosen Publishing has developed an online list of Web sites related to the subject of this book. This site is updated regularly. Please use this link to access the list:

http://www.rosenlinks.com/dcb/cbbg

FOR FURTHER READING

Castro, Elizabeth. *Publishing a Blog with Blogger*. Berkeley, CA: Peachpit Press, 2005.

Greenspan, Philip. *Philip and Alex's Guide to Web Publishing*. Retrieved December 5, 2006 (http://philip.greenspun.com/panda/).

Hewitt, Hugh. *Blog, Understanding the Information Reformation That's Changing Your World*. Nashville, TN: Nelson Business, 2005.

Hill, Brad. *Blogging for Dummies*. Indianapolis, IN: Wiley Publishing, Inc., 2006.

Jenkins, Henry. "Confronting the Challenges of Participatory Culture: Media Education for the 21st Century." MacArthur Foundation. 2006. Retrieved February 5, 2007 (http://www.macfound. org/site/c.lkLXJ8MQKrH/b.1038727/apps/s/ content.asp?ct = 2946895).

Pogue, David. "Wonkette's Ingredients for a Successful Blog." *New York Times*, July 26, 2006. Retrieved July 30, 2006 (http://www.nytimes.com/2006/ 07/26/technology/27PGOUE-EMAIL. html?pagewanted = print).

Risdahl, Aliza Sherman. *The Everything Blogging Book*. Avon, MA: Adams Media, 2006.

Stone, Biz. *Blogging: Genius Strategies for Instant Web Content*. Berkeley, CA: New Riders Press, 2002.

BIBLIOGRAPHY

Bausch, Paul, Matthew Haughey, and Meg Hourihan. *We Blog: Publishing Online with Weblogs*. Indianapolis, IN: Wiley Publishing, Inc., 2002.

Blood, Rebecca. *The Weblog Handbook: Practical Advice on Creating and Maintaining Your Blog*. New York, NY: Perseus Books Group, 2002.

"Creative Commons." Wikipedia. From an article entitled "Founder's Copyright" retrieved on April 7, 2006. Retrieved November 20, 2006 (http://en.wikipedia.org/wiki/Creative_commons#_note-1).

Dewar, James A. "The Digital Age and the Printing Press: Looking Backward to See Ahead." Retrieved November 2, 2006 (http://web.rollins.edu/~tlairson/tech/printpress.pdf).

Gosney, John. *Blogging for Teens*. Boston, MA: Thomson Course Technology, 2004.

Lenhart, Amanda, and Susannah Fox. *Bloggers: A Portrait of the Internet's New Storytellers*. Washington, DC: Pew Internet & American Life Project, 2006.

Masterson, Katheryn. "MySpace, MyStage: Who Needs a Record Deal? Artist Can Now Sell Their Music Directly Through MySpace?" *Chicago Tribune-RedEye*, October 5, 2006. Retrieved December 12, 2006 (http://www.futureofmusicbook.com/2006/10/myspace_mystage.html).

"New Republic Suspends an Editor for Attacks on Blog," *New York Times*, September 4, 2006, p. C-4.

Risdahl, Aliza Sherman. *The Everything Blogging Book*. Avon, MA: Adams Media, 2006.

Richardson, Will. *Blogs, Wikis, Podcasts and Other Powerful Web Tools for Classrooms*. Thousand Oaks, CA: Corwin Press, 2006.

Thompson, Clive. "Blogs to Riches: The Haves and Have-Nots of the Blogging Boom." *New York*, February 20, 2006.Retrieved January 4, 2007 (http://nymag.com/news/media/15967/).

Wakeman, Denise, and Patsi Krakoff. "Sixteen Ways to Drive Traffic to Your Blog." EzineArticles. March 25, 2005. Retrieved December 13, 2006 (http://www.ezinearticles.com/?16-Ways-to-Drive-Traffic-to-Your-Blog&id=22928).

INDEX

About the Author

Deirdre Day-MacLeod, Ph.D., has been blogging about all sorts of odd things since 2001. She has made every mistake a blogger can make on My Life as a Rabid Blog (deirdedaymacleod.blogspot.com), but nevertheless has been hired as a professional blogger. She has published fiction, essays, music reviews, and interviews on popular Web sites. Her work in traditional media has appeared in such publications as the *New York Times*, *Seventeen*, and *Women's Studies Quarterly*. She has published two books on Mexico and has edited or ghostwritten many others. She has taught writing and literature at a college level and holds a doctorate in English from the City University of New York and a master's in fiction writing from New York University.

Photo Credits

Cover, pp. 1, 27 iStockphoto; p. 4 DARPA; p. 7 © Christopher Coulter; p. 10 © AFP/Getty Images; p. 16 James Duncan Davidson/O'Reilly Media; p. 19 NewsCom; p. 28 © AP/Wide World Photos; p. 32 Shutterstock; p. 46 © Ryan McVay/Photodisc/Getty Images.

Designer: Nelson Sá; **Photo Researcher:** Marty Levick